Issues and Insights
from the Army Technology Seminar Game

Richard Darilek, Bruce Pirnie, Steve Drezner, Leland Joe, John Gordon IV, Walter Perry

T0159551

Prepared for the United States Army
Approved for public release; distribution unlimited

Arroyo Center

RAND

The research described in this report was sponsored by the United States Army under Contract No. DASW01-96-C-0004.

Library of Congress Cataloging-in-Publication Data

Issues and insights from the Army Technology Seminar Game / Richard Darilek ... [et al.].
    p. cm.
    Includes bibliographical references.
    "MR-1299."
    ISBN 0-8330-2972-X
    1. United States. Army. 2. Military art and science—Technological innovations.
3. Army Technology Seminar Game (1998 : Carlisle, Pa.) 4. War games. I.
Darilek, Richard E.

    UA25 .I87 2002
    355'.07—dc21

2001020493

RAND is a nonprofit institution that helps improve policy and decisionmaking through research and analysis. RAND® is a registered trademark. RAND's publications do not necessarily reflect the opinions or policies of its research sponsors.

(The cover image courtesy of The Boeing Company)

Published 2001 by RAND
1700 Main Street, P.O. Box 2138, Santa Monica, CA 90407-2138
1200 South Hayes Street, Arlington, VA 22202-5050
201 North Craig Street, Suite 102, Pittsburgh, PA 15213-1516
RAND URL: http://www.rand.org/
To order RAND documents or to obtain additional information,
contact Distribution Services: Telephone: (310) 451-7002;
Fax: (310) 451-6915; Internet: order@rand.org

The Chief of Staff of the Army initiated the Army After Next (AAN) Project in February 1996 under the leadership of the Training and Doctrine Command (TRADOC). The AAN goals were to link Army XXI to a long-term vision of the Army extending well into the 21st century and to ensure that this vision informed evolving Army research and development requirements.

In support of the AAN Project, the Assistant Secretary of the Army for Research, Development, and Acquisition (SARDA)—since renamed the Assistant Secretary of the Army for Acquisition, Logistics and Technology (ASA(ALT))—sponsored the Army Technology Seminar Game (ATSG), held at the Army War College in Carlisle, Pennsylvania from July 27 to July 31, 1998. Ensuring close correspondence between research and force requirements is a critical challenge for the U.S. Army in an era of rapid technological progress. To meet this challenge, the ATSG brought together civilian technologists and military operators. RAND Arroyo Center was asked to observe the ATSG, identify major issues emerging from the game, and provide an assessment. This report documents outcomes of this research. A follow-on technology game was conducted in July of 1999. This game was identified as the Technology and Materiel Game—TMG. It incorporated many of the recommendations summarized in the report.

The AAN process has since been superseded by the Transformation Campaign Plan, which envisions the creation of Brigade Combat Teams equipped with an Interim Armored Vehicle. By 2005, the Army plans to have a brigade that could be airlifted anywhere in the world within 96 hours. Subsequently, the Army plans to develop and field the Objective Force equipped with a new family of vehicles, but decisions on the Objective Force will be highly dependent upon technological progress.

During the ATSG, SARDA asked the Arroyo Center to track and analyze the game's outcomes from a "system-of-systems" perspective. In responding to this request, we developed three overarching "systems-of-systems" or "metasystems," i.e., Operations, C4ISR, and Logistics, that were subsequently adopted by the sponsor. These "systems-of-systems" helped the sponsor to capture, organize, and elucidate the game's outcomes.[1] However, reviewers of our initial draft of this document found the terminology "systems-of-systems" and "metasystems" to be unfamiliar and even confusing. In response to their concerns, we abandoned these terms and adopted instead a hierarchy of component, system, and function, as defined in this report. Operations, C4ISR, and Logistics are thus classified as functions, rather than "systems-of-systems."

The Arroyo Center has previously reported on the AAN process, for example in Walter L. Perry et al., *Issues Raised During the Army After Next Spring Wargame*, MR-1023-A, 1999. This research should be of interest to anyone concerned with the development of Army forces.

The research effort that produced this document was carried out in RAND Arroyo Center's Force Development and Technology Program. The Arroyo Center is a federally funded research and development center sponsored by the United States Army.

For more information on the RAND Arroyo Center, contact the Director of Operations, (310) 393-0411, extension 6500, or visit the Arroyo Center's Web site at http://www.rand.org/organization/ard/

---

[1]See, for example, U.S. Army, *1998 Army Technology Seminar Game Report*, Assistant Secretary of the Army for Research, Development, and Acquisition, published by Science Applications International Corporation, Washington, D.C., 1999.

CONTENTS

FIGURES

SUMMARY

The Army Technology Seminar Game (ATSG) was designed to advance the Army After Next (AAN) process by bringing together military operators and civilian scientists and technologists to examine issues of importance to future force development. The ATSG was a combination of seminar and wargame. It resembled a seminar in that there was no play of opposing forces and no consequences for players' decisions. It resembled a game in using "vignettes," i.e., short scenarios derived from recent AAN wargames. The players were presented these vignettes and a set of notional military systems. For each vignette, they were asked to discuss what systems might be most useful and finally to vote for systems.

FUNCTIONS

Players usually debated at the levels of components and systems, seldom at the level of functions. But functions imply combinations of systems with obvious implications for the individual systems. For example, a light armored vehicle and a transport rotorcraft might be developed in harmony to support an air-mechanized concept.

The RAND Arroyo Center team raised analysis to the functional level by examining how players' decisions affect the performance of functions. For example, the players might examine an Advanced Airframe and associated technologies such as high-performance turbine engine, signature reduction, and advanced rotors. Their decisions might have an impact on combinations of the Advanced Airframe and Advanced Attack Airframe with AAN Vehicles to support an air-mechanized concept.

The Arroyo Center team also attempted to map technologies to functions. In total, Arroyo analysts identified 426 separate technologies[2] listed on the System Cards, including modifications during the game. Of these, 143 supported C4ISR, 244 supported Operations, and 156 supported Logistics.

PLAYERS' INSIGHTS

Because of time pressure, the players could not analyze issues that emerged during the game. But despite these limitations, their informed discussion generated many useful insights.

Combat Land Vehicles

The important issues concerned close combat and mobility. Most players tended to believe that close combat would be inescapable, and many doubted that vehicles in the 15-ton class would have sufficient protection to engage in such combat successfully. The game raised two kinds of mobility issues: global deployment and maneuver in theater. Players thought that Army After Next Vehicle lifted by an Advanced Airframe would enjoy advantages in global deployment, but they were not certain that a force built on these systems could maneuver successfully against a sophisticated air defense.

C4ISR

The players discussed a wide variety of C4ISR systems during the game, especially Information Warfare System, Military Operations in Urban Terrain (MOUT) Sensor Package, Tactical Internet Hardware, Defensive Information Warfare, Advanced Situational Awareness System, Advanced Command and Control System, Future Common Engagement System, and Tactical Information Infrastructure. They recognized that most of these systems were interrelated and should not be developed or fielded in isolation. They thought that the

---

[2]System Cards identified 1,147 "critical enabling technologies," but some of the entries were redundant. After resolving the redundancies, we compiled the list offered in Appendix A.

commercial world is driving development of information technology, but not always in ways suitable for military application.

"Iron Mountain"

Players were strongly interested in ways to make logistics support less cumbersome without incurring operational risks. They were skeptical about just-in-time logistics because requirements are inherently unpredictable and the consequences of wrong estimates could be catastrophic. But they believed that the Army currently tends to accumulate overly large stockpiles in theater, the so-called "iron mountain." They were especially interested in two systems: Combat Service Support/Logistics Information System (CSS/LIS) and Flexible Adjustable Modular Packaging.

FUTURE DIRECTIONS

The ATSG surfaced issues relating to technology and future systems, but it did not produce results that could inform Army research and development. To accomplish this goal, the Army needs to embed technology seminar games in a more comprehensive process. At the start of the process, Training and Doctrine Command (TRADOC) should use the Army's missions to derive a statement of desired capabilities. Then the ASA(ALT) should produce lists of current and potentially available technologies that appear relevant. The ATSG should be a "brainstorming" session to project systems that would attain the desired capabilities by exploiting technologies. Specific scenarios are too distracting and confining for an exercise of this kind. It would be better to work simply from a statement of desired capabilities. TRADOC should sponsor force-building seminars that envision alternative future forces using the projected systems according to reasonably well-defined operational concepts, i.e., visions of how to employ the systems effectively. Finally, TRADOC should evaluate these future forces through wargaming.

ABBREVIATIONS

AAAF	Advanced Attack Airframe
AAN	Army After Next
AAF	Advanced Airframe
AANV	Army After Next Vehicles
A-FOG-M	Advanced Fiber-Optic Guided Missile
ASA(ALT)	Assistant Secretary of the Army (Acquisition, Logistics and Technology)
ATACMS	Army Tactical Missile System
ATSG	Army Technology Seminar Game
AUAV- A	AAN Unmanned Aerial Vehicle-A
BM	ballistic missile
C4ISR	command, control, communications, computers, intelligence, surveillance, and reconnaissance
CM	cruise missile
CSS/LIS	Combat Service Support/Logistics Information System
DNA	deoxyribonucleic acid
EMP	electromagnetic pulse
EW	electronic warfare

FGV	Future Ground Vehicles
GPS	Global Positioning System
HUMS	Health and Usage Monitoring System
IFF	identification friend or foe
IHPT	Integrated High Performance Turbine
JTAGG	Joint Turbine Advanced Gas Generator
JTR-H	Joint Transport Rotorcraft–Helicopter
JTR-T	Joint Transport Rotorcraft–Tilt Rotor
METT-T-C	mission, enemy, troops, terrain–time–control
MEU	Marine Expeditionary Unit
MLRS	Multiple Launch Rocket System
MOUT	military operations in urban terrain
NEO	noncombatant evacuation operation
NGO	nongovernmental organization
SAIC	Science Applications International Corporation
SARDA	Assistant Secretary of the Army for Research, Development, and Acquisition (predecessor of ASA(ALT))
TOPKAT	Tele-Operated Precision Kill and Targeting Missile
TRADOC	Training and Doctrine Command
UAV	unmanned aerial vehicle
WMD	weapons of mass destruction

Chapter One

INTRODUCTION

The Army Technology Seminar Game (ATSG) was designed to advance the Army After Next (AAN) process by bringing together military operators and civilian scientists and technologists to examine issues of importance to future force development. The rationale behind the game's organization has been most clearly articulated by former Secretary of Defense William J. Perry: "The Army stands to benefit greatly from dialogue between disparate communities of military officers with field experience and civilian scientists and engineers with experience in research and development. Military officers can envision what capabilities they will need and how they would apply these capabilities in various environments. Civilian researchers can envision how applied science and technology could help to achieve these capabilities."[1]

The Army Technology Seminar Game had three main objectives:

- Identify the most promising technologies to satisfy AAN force objectives.

- Support the Defense Industrial Base Strategy for technology investments and production of AAN systems.

- Support AAN, Army Vision 2010, and Joint Vision 2010 force developments.

---

[1]William J. Perry, during the plenary session of the Army Technology Seminar Game.

GAME DESIGN

The ATSG was a combination of seminar and wargame. It resembled a seminar in that there was no play of opposing forces and no consequences for players' decisions. It resembled a game in using "vignettes," i.e., short scenarios derived from recent AAN wargames. (See Appendix B for a sample vignette.) The players were presented these vignettes and a set of notional military systems. For each vignette, they were asked to discuss what systems might be most useful and finally to vote for systems.

Vignettes

The ATSG employed fifteen vignettes derived from previous AAN wargames. Each vignette included a descriptive title, a brief statement of the situation, a mission for U.S. forces, data on opposing forces, and associated issues. For example, the vignette entitled "Road to War" featured an insurgent organization in Sumatra that had acquired two nuclear weapons. U.S. forces had the mission of seizing the weapons against opposition from forces that ranged from regular troops to a covert terrorist organization. The issues included coordination with allies and a nonpermissive noncombatant evacuation operation (NEO).

Systems

Systems (represented by "System Cards") were notional end items of military equipment, e.g., an armored vehicle. Each system included a name, a brief description, a column headed "Critical Enabling Technology," and entries associated with both conservative and aggressive approaches to research and development. For example, one System Card presented Army After Next Vehicles (AANV) and described a family of advanced tactical vehicles that included variants for command and control, fire support, reconnaissance, etc. The column "Critical Enabling Technology" was actually a list of components such as gun/missile, propulsion, survivability (active and passive protection), etc. The conservative approach to gun/missile offered a non-line-of-sight missile, an electrothermal gun, Hellfire II, and Stinger. The aggressive approach offered a compact kinetic energy missile and an electromagnetic gun.

The players began with a set of System Cards provided by the organizers. These cards focused on systems that would support the air-mechanized force played in previous AAN wargames. Players were not limited to this original set of System Cards. On the contrary, they were encouraged to revise System Cards and to develop entirely new ones. Finally, they voted on System Cards, thereby indicating which systems they considered useful in the context of each vignette. They were not required to justify their decisions, but they often gave rationales during open discussions. RAND Arroyo Center observers attempted to capture these arguments in their field notes. Since the discussions were held under considerable time pressure, these arguments were often fragmentary or sketchy.

Sequence of Events

The ATSG followed the sequence of events shown graphically in Figure 1.1:

1. Players scanned vignettes that implied a need for certain *capabilities*.

2. Players examined System Cards that depicted *systems* and *technologies*.

3. Players discussed the usefulness of candidate systems, revised System Cards, and added new System Cards.

4. Players voted on all relevant System Cards in context of the vignettes.

5. The teams, a senior review group, Science Applications International Corporation (SAIC), and RAND Arroyo Center reviewed and analyzed players' discussions during the seminar game and their votes for System Cards.

System Cards were thus the fundamental component of the game. They linked systems and technologies in a one-to-many relationship, and they linked both systems and technologies to the required force capabilities.

RAND*MR1299-1.1*

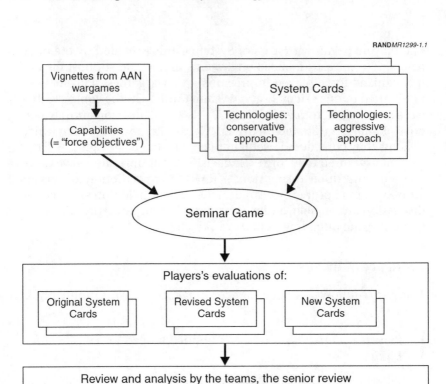

Figure 1.1—Structure of the Technology Seminar Game

LINKAGES AMONG CAPABILITIES, SYSTEMS, AND TECHNOLOGIES

Although systems and technologies remained inextricably linked
through the System Cards, the game proceeded from capabilities to
systems to technologies. In this sense, it might be broadly characterized as "capabilities push." But the reverse sequence of "technology
push" is also valid. In this sequence, technology suggests systems
that are evaluated according to their ability to generate required
capabilities. In the real world, both sequences occur simultaneously
and are dynamically interrelated. (See Figure 1.2.)

Systems are in a central position, defined simultaneously by demands for capability and the ability of technology to satisfy those demands. Scientists and technicians in the civilian world and even within military research and development may achieve breakthroughs for which the military utility is not immediately obvious. At the same time, military officers may identify demands that cannot be met by existing systems, no matter how cleverly employed. This is because demands for capability are essentially insatiable. An ideal combat vehicle kills all opposing systems, is impervious to enemy response, moves close to the speed of light, and is imperceptible. But an actual combat vehicle kills some opposing systems, has some degree of protection, moves at severely constrained speeds, and is often detected.

RAND*MR1299-1.2*

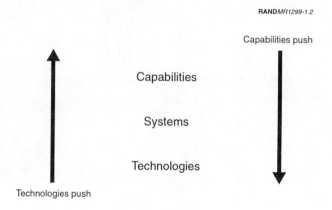

Figure 1.2—Capabilities, Systems, Technologies

Chapter Two

FUNCTIONAL PERSPECTIVE

During the Army Technology Seminar Game, RAND Arroyo Center was asked to examine play from a wider perspective than players were able to adopt. Arroyo Center analysts grouped those systems examined during the game into functional areas and discerned the impact of players' decisions on the performance of these functions.

DEFINITIONS

The ATSG was built around System Cards, each describing a notional system that the Army might develop in the future. For example, one System Card described "Army After Next Vehicles," a family of lightly armored, C-130 transportable combat vehicles optimized for close combat, fire support, reconnaissance, command and control, etc. The first column of data on a System Card was headed "Critical Enabling Technology." However, most entries under this column were actually components of the system. For example, the components of "AAN Vehicles" were gun/missile, propulsion, survivability, systems integration, sensors, and structure. The next two columns, headed "Conservative Approach" and "Aggressive Approach" had entries that variously alluded to technology (e.g., "Proton Exchange Membrane Fuel Cell"), existing equipment (e.g., "Improved Stinger"), and performance goals (e.g., "signature reduction"). Partially as a result of this ambiguity, players tended to be imprecise in their language. For the sake of clarity, the following definitions are used throughout this report:

Component: major assembly within a system. For example, gun/missile, propulsion, survivability suite, automated integration, sensors, and structure were components of AAN Vehicles.

System: major item of equipment, for example, AAN Vehicle, Future Ground Vehicle, High-Mobility Follower, Cross-Country Racer Fighting Vehicle. In most cases these were the items displayed on System Cards during the ATSG.

Function: overarching rationale for combining systems. The Arroyo Center team grouped systems under three functions: C4ISR, Operations, and Logistics.

RAND ARROYO CENTER APPROACH

Players usually debated at the levels of components and systems, seldom at the level of functions. But functional combinations of systems have obvious implications for the individual systems. For example, a light armored vehicle and a transport rotorcraft might be developed in harmony to support an air-mechanized concept.

The Arroyo Center team raised analysis to the functional level by examining the impact of players' decisions on the performance of functions. For example, the players might examine an Advanced Airframe and associated technologies such as high-performance turbine engine, signature reduction, and advanced rotors. Their decisions might have an impact on combinations of the Advanced Airframe and Advanced Attack Airframe with AAN Vehicles to support an air-mechanized concept.

The Arroyo Center team also attempted to map technologies to functions. In total, Arroyo analysts identified 426 separate technologies[1] listed on the System Cards, including modifications during the game. Of these, 143 supported C4ISR, 244 supported Operations, and 156 supported Logistics.

---

[1]System Cards identified 1,147 "critical enabling technologies," but some of the entries were redundant. After resolving redundancies, we compiled the list offered in Appendix A.

C4ISR

The C4ISR area included all systems that contributed to achieving situational awareness for friendly forces and denying it to opposing forces. Within this area, Arroyo Center analysts identified three subfunctions: collection systems, transmission systems, and user systems. These are defined as follows.

- **Collection systems** provide information that contributes to situational awareness. These include sensor and source systems and fusion algorithms.

- **Transmission systems** carry the information from source to destination throughout the area of operations. These are primarily communications networks that constitute a connectivity grid.

- **User systems** support the users of information.

Figure 2.1 summarizes technology overlaps within C4ISR. Of the 142 systems that could be considered C4ISR technologies, 32 support more than one C4ISR subfunction. See Appendix A for a complete listing of all C4ISR systems annotated to reflect applicability across all subareas.

C4ISR System Cards

System Cards associated with C4ISR included the following: AAN Unmanned Aerial Vehicle (UAV), Micro UAV, Biological Remote Early Warning System, Chemical Remote Early Warning System, Information Warfare System, Laser Communications, Automatic Target Recognition Package, MOUT Sensor Package, Tactical Internet Hardware, Near-Real-Time Surveillance in Pod, Conventional Electromagnetic Pulse Generator, Defense Information Warfare, Advanced Situational Awareness System, Advanced Command and Control System, Future Common Engagement System, Tactical Information Infrastructure, RF Information Disrupter, Ground-Based Laser Anti-Satellite System, and Space-Based Communications.

The players recognized that these systems were related, some of them so closely that they should be developed together. In particu-

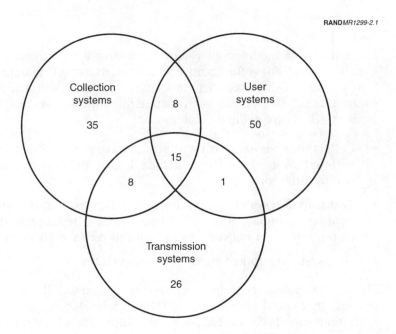

RAND*MR1299-2.1*

Figure 2.1—C4ISR System Overlaps

lar, they thought the Automatic Target Recognition Package, MOUT Sensor Package, Tactical Internet Hardware, Advanced Situational Awareness System, Advanced Command and Control System, Future Common Engagement System, and Tactical Information Infrastructure should be fully compatible and mutually supporting. However, game design promoted consideration of individual systems and offered no opportunity to develop groups of systems.

Players' Evaluation of C4ISR

In general, the players thought the commercial world would lead development of information technology, and the Army should be able to exploit this development without investing much of its own money. However, the Army should also exercise caution because open architecture is accessible to prospective opponents and not immune to failure. For example, one ATSG player recounted that the Navy had suffered crashes traceable to the widely available commercial program Windows NT that incapacitated entire ships. Players generally supposed that very large amounts of data would be constantly available, but that each formation, unit, or individual would require only limited amounts of it. They considered definition of data requirements to be a difficult problem that is nowhere near solution. In addition, some players thought that data fusion might present serious difficulties. There was general skepticism that by the year 2020 unit commanders would have complete oversight of the battlefield, including locations of friendly and known enemy forces.

OPERATIONS

Operations included all systems that contributed to defeating enemy forces in contact with or near friendly forces. The largest number of systems fell into one of the three following categories: mobility, lethality, and survivability. A total of 244 technologies supported Operational Systems in all categories: 53 supported mobility, 81 supported lethality, and 122 supported survivability. Figure 2.2 illustrates the overlaps within this function. See Appendix A for a complete listing of all systems annotated to reflect applicability across all subareas.

Operational System Cards

Lethal systems included: Advanced Airframe, Advanced Attack Airframe, Joint Transport Rotorcraft-Helicopter, Joint Transport Rotorcraft-Tilt Rotor, Lift UAVs, AAN UAVs, Robotic Airlifter, AAN Vehicles, Future Ground Vehicles, Cross-Country Racer Fighting Vehicle, Last-Ditch Air Defense System, Advanced Fiber-Optic Guided Missile, Firestorm, Point Hit Multiple Launch Rocket System (MLRS), Low-Cost Precision Kill Rocket, Tele-Operated Precision Kill and Targeting Missile, Blaster Anti-Armor System, Advanced Light Anti-Armor System, Advanced Fire Support System, Advanced Light Machine Gun, Individual Assault Gun, Wide Area Mine and Control System, Land Warrior for AAN, Advanced Airdrop, Theater Missile Defense System, and Space-Based Fire Support.

Nonlethal systems would have utility against an opponent employing hugging tactics and in all situations involving noncombatants. Nonlethal systems included: Non-Lethal Small Arms Munitions

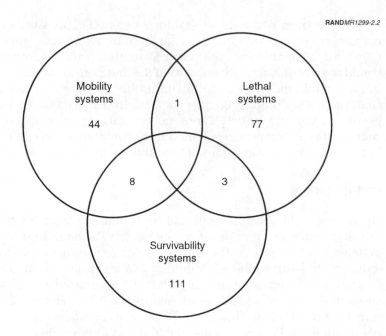

RAND*MR1299-2.2*

Figure 2.2—Operational System Overlaps

Systems, Non-Lethal Ground and Vehicle Launched Munitions, Non-Lethal Vehicle and Vessel Disablers, and Non-Lethal Area-Denial Barriers.

Rival Concepts

Air-mechanized concept. Within this function, the game offered a set of System Cards that embodied a particular operational concept, namely the air-mechanized concept played in AAN wargames. These systems included:[2]

- Advanced Airframe: tilt-rotor aircraft capable of lifting 15-ton vehicles

---

[2]There was a System Card for "Army After Next UAVs." But apart from the name it was not clear why these UAVs should be associated more closely with Army After Next Vehicles than with Future Ground Vehicles.

- Advanced Attack Airframe: tilt-rotor aircraft carrying weapons

- Army After Next Vehicles: 7.5- to 15-ton combat and combat support vehicles

- Advanced Fire Support System: anti-armor munitions in unattended pods

- Advanced Air Drop: delivery of precision munitions and sensors.

Players recognized that these systems were related. For example, they noted that the Advanced Airframe and the Advanced Attack Airframe shared not only tilt-rotor technology but also had identical speed and range, creating a presumption that they would operate together. The Advanced Airframe was clearly designed to lift the Army After Next Vehicles. The Advanced Fire Support System seemed intended to support forces at operational depth that lacked intrinsic firepower. Logically, players should have evaluated these systems together as one concept, but game rules required evaluation by system.

Light armor concept. Within the operational area, the game offered one System Card that suggested a light armor concept: the Future Ground Vehicles. These 20-ton vehicles offered greater protection than the AAN Vehicles but were not airmobile, i.e., they exceeded the lift capability of the Advanced Airframe. A light armor concept was not fully developed, but the Future Ground Vehicles might have been associated with Fast Ships capable of deploying forces 9,000 nautical miles in five days.

Rival Systems

Within this function, there were sets of rivals, i.e., systems competing so directly that the Army would be unlikely to build both. One set was the Army After Next Vehicles versus the Future Ground Vehicles. In addition, there were several sets of rival systems offering fire support:

- Advanced Fiber-Optic Guided Missile (A-FOG-M) with a 50-kilometer range and built-in identification friend or foe (IFF) versus Tele-Operated Precision Kill and Targeting Missile (TOPKAT) with a 30-kilometer range and Automatic Target Recognition, both using fiber-optic technology.

- Low-Cost Precision Kill Rocket, a precision-guided anti-tank rocket with a 6-kilometer range and Automatic Target Recognition, versus Blaster, a compact guided hypervelocity missile with a 5-kilometer range.

More useful insights might have emerged if the players had viewed these systems as rivals and debated their relative merits, but the rules of the game required evaluations by system.

Players' Evaluation of Operations

Players thought that the fleet of Advanced Airframes required to implement an air-mechanized concept would be too costly, especially if the commercial world continues to evince little interest in very large tilt-rotor aircraft. In addition, some players thought that such aircraft would suffer significant problems in the transition between level and vertical flight regimes. The players were also highly skeptical about the combat power of Army After Next Vehicles that weighed only 15 tons. Most players thought that combat vehicles would have to weigh well over 20 tons to achieve a desirable degree of ballistic protection.

One of the major conclusions with regard to operations was that capabilities portrayed during the AAN Spring Wargame appeared unachievable using the airframes and ground vehicles portrayed in the ATSG System Cards. Instead, players recommended that the Army explore other approaches to achieving this capability.

LOGISTICS

Logistics included all systems that contributed to *deploying* forces at distance and *supporting* them in theater. A total of 156 technologies supported Logistics systems-of-systems in both categories: 68 supported deployability systems and 102 supported supportability systems. Figure 2.3 illustrates the interdependencies within this function. See Appendix A for a complete listing of all systems annotated to reflect applicability across all subareas.

RAND*MR1299-2.3*

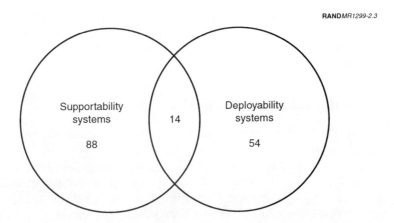

Figure 2.3—Logistics System Overlaps

Logistics System Cards

System Cards associated with Logistics included: Joint Transport Rotorcraft-Helicopter, Joint Transport Rotorcraft-Tilt Rotor, Lift UAVs, Robotic Airlifter High-Mobility Followers, Advanced Air Drop, Battle Space Energy Sources, Combat Service Support/Logistics Information System, Fast Ships, Flexible/Adjustable Modular Packaging, Modular Water Generation System, Vertical Deployable CHE/MHE, and Quick Logistics-Over-the-Shore.

Rival Systems

Within the logistics area, there were rivals, i.e., systems competing so directly that the Army would be unlikely to build both:

- Joint Transport Rotorcraft–Helicopter (JTR-H) versus Joint Transport Rotorcraft–Tilt Rotor (JTR-T), both having a 2,100-nautical-mile range, a 10-ton payload, and a 30mm cannon. Tactical speed differed significantly: 175 knots for JTR-H versus 320 knots for JTR-T.

Players recognized this rivalry and discussed to some extent the relative merits of the two systems. There was disagreement on the technical risk of a large tilt-rotor program and the utility of increased speed. Some players thought that greater speed would increase survivability, while others thought it made little difference against modern low-level air defenses.

Players' Evaluation of Logistics

Players tended to consider logistics systems individually rather than as performing a broad function. Their attention focused on strategic lifters, including Fast Ships, Quick Logistics-Over-the-Shore, and two new System Cards developed during the game: New Conventional Aircraft and Rigid Airship. Regarding Fast Ships, players thought that increased trafficability and sea state mitigation would be important. One means to mitigate sea state might be a rapidly deployable breakwater, analogous to the breakwaters used during the Normandy landings in World War II. They conceived a New Conventional Aircraft using high-bypass turbofans and interchangeable pods to deliver cargo. They also conceived a Rigid Airship with intercontinental range and a million-pound payload, but they doubted whether such a system could operate safely in poor weather. For all these systems, they thought that commercial interest would be an important, perhaps vitally important, variable because the Army could not afford to fund much development in this area within its expected budgets.

OVERLAP OF FUNCTIONS

Functions are obviously not discrete. On the contrary, they overlap extensively, with regard to both systems and their associated technologies. Figures 2.1 through 2.3 illustrated the overlaps within each function; however, there is considerable overlap among functions. For example, decision aids concern operations as well as C4ISR. Indeed, they epitomize the close linkage between these functions. Radio frequency tags are applicable to both the C4ISR function and the logistics function. The Global Positioning System (GPS) has applications in all three functional areas. Figure 2.4 illustrates these overlaps. Critical technologies and technologies that offer especially great leverage are apt to be found where functions overlap. See Appendix A for a complete listing of all systems annotated to reflect applicability across all subareas.

RAND*MR1299-2.4*

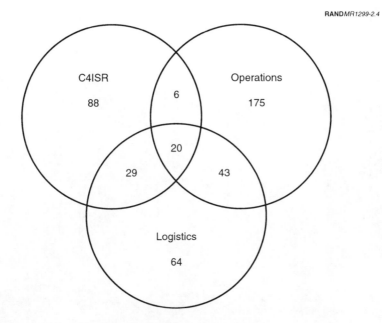

Figure 2.4—Functional Area Overlaps

Chapter Three

MAJOR ISSUES AND INSIGHTS

Because of time pressure, the players could not analyze issues that emerged during the game. Despite these limitations, their informed discussion generated many useful insights. This chapter highlights the most significant issues that emerged during the game and insights offered by the players. These are grouped under the corresponding functions: Operations, C4ISR, and Logistics.

OPERATIONAL ISSUES AND INSIGHTS

Operations includes all those systems that directly contribute to defeat of enemy forces in a theater of operations. In the context of the ATSG, the most important operational systems were combat vehicles and related aircraft. These included the Advanced Airframe (AAF) with a 15-ton payload, the 15-ton Army After Next Vehicles (AANV) that were AAF transportable, and the 20-ton Future Ground Vehicles (FGV) that were not AAF transportable.

Combat Land Vehicles

The important issues concerned close combat and mobility. Most players tended to believe that close combat would be inescapable, and many doubted that vehicles in the 15-ton class would have sufficient protection to engage successfully in such combat. The game raised two kinds of mobility issues: global deployment and maneuver in theater. Players thought that AANV lifted by AAF would enjoy advantages in global deployment, but they were not certain that a force built on these systems could maneuver successfully against a sophisticated air defense.

Protection. Should a future force be capable of engaging in close combat? If so, how much passive protection would be required and how much would this protection weigh? To what extent would active protection be a viable alternative? Players produced these insights:

- Most players believed that at least some close combat would be inescapable. They thought that if Army forces maneuvered in close proximity to opposing forces, some contact would be unavoidable if only because situational awareness was imperfect. If, on the other hand, Army forces stayed away from opposing forces, then they appeared to duplicate capabilities already offered by air forces and special operations forces.

- Most players thought that the degree of passive protection provided in a 15-ton AANV would be insufficient to accept close combat. (AANV were armored against small arms at any range and machine guns beyond 500 meters.) To make a vehicle in this weight class viable, the Army would need either a breakthrough in armor technology or active protection against ballistic weapons. However, the players were skeptical that "bullet-against-bullet" types of protection would be feasible.

- Players noted that a 20-ton AFV would have a higher degree of protection at the expense of not being transportable by AAF.

Global deployment. Should the Army develop self-deployable systems? What alternatives should be considered? Players produced these insights:

- Players thought that rapid global deployment was a vital requirement for Army forces, but they were generally skeptical about developing self-deployable systems, considering the weight restriction on combat vehicles and high costs, both for procurement and for subsequent support.

- Players discussed several alternatives to self-deployability, including a new airlifter and fast sealift. (See the discussion of logistics below.)

Maneuver. Could a force built on AANV/AAF maneuver successfully against an opponent with a sophisticated air defense? Could FGV maneuver fast enough and in sufficient depth?

- Players generally believed that the Army would require greater in-theater mobility, but they doubted that AANV/AAF could survive over enemy-held terrain. They thought that stealth was impossible in a large tilt-rotor aircraft and that these aircraft would be vulnerable to short-range air defense missiles, even after the Air Force suppressed surveillance radars. To conduct such maneuver successfully, the Army would need a high degree of active protection against air defense missiles.

- As an alternative, players considered FGV with a dash speed of 100 kilometers per hour as depicted on the System Card. Some players thought that speed in this range to depths of several hundred kilometers would be adequate in most theaters of operations. There was debate as to whether a 20-ton FGV should be wheeled or tracked. Wheels offered greater speed and ease of maintenance, while tracks generally provided superior off-road mobility.

Combat Aerial Vehicles

The game offered two radically different types of combat aerial vehicles: Advanced Attack Airframe (AAAF) armed with cannon, Sidewinder, and Hellfire, and AAN Unmanned Aerial Vehicle-A (AUAV- A), armed with a kinetic energy missile, electronic warfare (EW) systems, and a microwave weapon directed against opposing electronic systems. AAAF was conceptually linked to the AANV/AAF team.

What kinds of combat aerial vehicles should the Army develop other than attack helicopters?

- Players were highly critical of the AAAF. They thought that an attack platform should be smaller and stealthier than the tilt-rotor aircraft described in the System Card. They also considered the armament too conservative. Some players thought that rotary-wing aircraft, possibly a further development of Cheyenne, would be more effective than AAAF.

- Players saw more promise in AUAV-A if it could be developed and fielded at a reasonable cost. However, they continued to see UAV primarily in the surveillance role, providing data to deep-fire systems and attack aircraft.

Precision Munitions

Players generally devoted less attention to precision munitions than they did to combat land vehicles and aerial vehicles. However, they discussed several systems in this category, including Advanced Fiber-Optic Guided Missile, Point Hit Multiple Launch Rocket System, and Low-Cost Precision Kill Rocket. They were skeptical of the requirement set in one vignette to attack some 7,000 targets quickly, but they generally believed that the Army would require precision munitions in considerable numbers.

What kinds of precision munitions does the Army need?

- Players generally believed that the Army should be able to attack with considerable precision and in great depth. Among the likely missions, they envisioned suppression of opposing air defense without risk to friendly aircraft.

- Some players thought that the technologies depicted in the System Cards were too conservative and that advances in microprocessing would make new approaches feasible. They expected that new technologies might be available even within the Army XXI timeframe.

C4ISR ISSUES AND INSIGHTS

The players discussed a wide variety of C4ISR systems during the game, especially Information Warfare System, MOUT Sensor Package, Tactical Internet Hardware, Defensive Information Warfare, Advanced Situational Awareness System, Advanced Command and Control System, Future Common Engagement System, and Tactical Information Infrastructure. They recognized that most of these systems were interrelated and should not be developed or fielded in isolation. They thought that the commercial world is driving development of information technology, but not always in ways suitable for military application.

Is the Army moving too slowly in information technology?

- Some players thought that the Army and the Defense Department are too slow to adopt commercial information technology. They noted that the commercial world develops and implements technology much faster than the military does. As a result, the Army lags behind the commercial world.

- Some players thought that business could always adopt and discard technologies more easily than the Army can because of the radically different requirements. Business requires commercial viability in a peaceful environment where the cost of failure might be merely a reduced profit margin. In strong contrast, the Army requires robust performance under sudden stress where the cost of failure might be death.

How should the Army take advantage of commercially developed information technologies?

- Players generally thought that the Army should take part in commercial information technology in order to identify payoffs and risks for military application.

- Several players noted that the Army and the Defense Department cannot simply adopt commercial information technology:

  — Even well-tested and widely used commercial software is subject to "crashes" that would be intolerable for military forces during war.

  — Future command and control systems will require robust capability for massively parallel processing greater than the commercial world is likely to develop.

What areas of information technology merit particular attention?

- Players agreed that the Army should devote attention to hardening against electromagnetic pulse (EMP). Force XXI will become increasingly dependent upon microprocessing, so much so that it could suffer catastrophic damage from EMP if its systems are insufficiently hardened. Even with hardening, the Army should have fallbacks in case automated information systems fail.

- Players were also alert to the risk of opposing information warfare, especially corruption of data transmissions. They noted that the Army and the Defense Department are becoming increasingly dependent on timely transmission of immense amounts of data, both administrative and operational. Interruption to this flow would be serious, but corruption poses an even greater risk.

LOGISTICS ISSUES AND INSIGHTS

During the game, players discussed a variety of aircraft options and the potential contribution of fast ships. They also discussed advantages to be obtained from near-real-time inventory control and modular packaging. In various contexts, they noted the Army's critical need for more efficient energy sources.

Aircraft Options

The players discussed a variety of aircraft options. These included Advanced Airframe (AAF), Joint Transport Rotorcraft–Helicopter (JTR-H), Joint Transport Rotorcraft–Tilt-Rotor (JTR-T), Lift UAV, and Common Air Transport (a C-17 class fixed-wing transport aircraft).

What aircraft type would best support global deployment? What are the advantages and disadvantages of procuring a fleet of large tilt-rotor aircraft?

- Players devoted special attention to AAF, a large tilt-rotor aircraft, because it would be able to lift AANV, thus realizing an air-mechanized concept. They tried to weigh pros and cons of developing and procuring such a system in large numbers.

  Players saw these advantages:

  — Global deployment within hours, independent of support other than aerial refueling. Army air-mechanized forces would thus have global mobility comparable or even superior to sister services.

  — High in-theater mobility to the extent that AAF could be refueled and avoid or suppress an opponent's short-range air defenses.

Players saw these disadvantages:

— High procurement cost, presumably at least $100 million per aircraft. Some players considered such aircraft unaffordable in sufficient numbers unless there were an unexpected increase in the Army's procurement budget.

— High support cost. Players had no specific figures in mind, but they anticipated that AAF would be expensive to maintain and would "guzzle" fuel.

— High signature due to the large rotors and high vulnerability to short-range air defense when used in an operational-tactical mode.

— Tight restriction on use. Players envisioned that AAF would be tightly bound to AANV and therefore unavailable to lift other loads.

— Difficulty transitioning between flight regimes.

• Players also considered a Common Air Transport, conceptually a C-17 class transport aircraft capable of lifting the 20-ton FGV. They generally believed that commercial interest would be essential to the economical development of a Common Air Transport. They discussed whether landing on unimproved landing strips would be required. In general, players believed that most regions of the world where the Army would be likely to operate would have a sufficiently large number of airports and runways.

• Players discussed the relative merits of JTR-H and JTR-T without evolving a clear preference for either of these competing systems.

• Developmental timelines were also cited as important issues for new aircraft. Several groups mentioned that for a major new aircraft to be available in quantity by 2020, it would have to be in production for a decade prior to that date.

Fast Ships

Players liked the Fast Ship, credited with 55 knots in the System Card. Some speculated that greater speeds might be feasible, possibly as high as 75 knots, but they were concerned by fuel consumption.

Players also worried about protection en route, the effects of high seas, vulnerability to sea mines, and offloading in the absence of modern port facilities. In addition, they were concerned about a lack of commercial interest in high speed at sea.

How much speed is achievable? What operational limitations would fast ships have?

- Some players speculated that a Fast Ship might attain as much as 75 knots using advanced hull design, but they were concerned that fuel consumption might be prohibitively high at such speeds. It might not be possible to refuel at sea, and refueling in port might negate higher speed.

- Players were uncertain about the requirement for protection en route. They noted that the Navy currently has no ships capable of such high speeds. However, some players believed that if high speed proved feasible, the Navy would almost certainly develop fast combatant ships in order to assure sea control.

- Players were skeptical about the ability of a Fast Ship to operate safely in high seas. They noted that strategically important areas of the world's oceans are subject to high sea states for major portions of the year.

- Players were considerably worried by the risk from sea mines, especially in straits and in the vicinity of port facilities. They noted the experience of the Persian Gulf, and some expressed doubt that the Navy was devoting sufficient resources to counter sea mines.

- Players were painfully aware that time gained in transit might be outweighed by time consumed in onloading and offloading. They were especially concerned about offloading without modern port facilities, either in their absence or because they were denied by an adversary.

- Players were not well informed about commercial interest, but they feared it might be insufficient to spur development of a Fast Ship suitable for military purposes. In the absence of commercial interest, they wondered if the Navy or Army would fund development.

"Iron Mountain"

Players were strongly interested in ways to make logistics support less cumbersome without incurring operational risks. They were skeptical about just-in-time logistics because requirements are inherently unpredictable, and the consequences of wrong estimates could be catastrophic. But they believed that the Army currently tends to accumulate overly large stockpiles in theater, the so-called "iron mountain." They were especially interested in two systems: Combat Service Support/Logistics Information System (CSS/LIS) and Flexible Adjustable Modular Packaging.

How can the Army make logistics support less cumbersome without incurring operational risks?

- Players thought that commercial advances in inventory control raised the prospect of near-real-time inventory control on a global basis, an immense improvement over previous performance. They saw improved inventory control as the key to reducing in-theater stocks to more manageable levels without risking shortages.

- Players saw modular packaging as another key to better performance in logistics. They thought such packaging could reduce handling times and loss or damage en route.

Energy Sources

Players thought that lighter and efficient power sources were a critical requirement. Their discussions focused on vehicular power sources and batteries to power man-portable systems.

How can the Army acquire more efficient energy sources?

- Players observed that the Army's man-portable systems are hampered or limited by battery technology. A soldier would have to carry prohibitive weight in batteries to power those systems that are currently feasible and useful to him. Therefore, lighter and more efficient batteries are a critical requirement.

- Players discussed vehicular fuels and engines at considerable length. They believed that the commercial world would take the lead in developing new technologies, but considerable militarization might be required. For example, future fuel, such as methane, might be too explosive for military use. Similarly, hydraulic systems operating at very great pressures might be too vulnerable to catastrophic failure under field conditions.

Chapter Four

FUTURE DIRECTIONS

In this chapter we outline a structure of seminars and wargames that would help achieve TRADOC's underlying purpose: to inform research and development leading to future forces that are more capable of accomplishing the Army's missions.

The ATSG surfaced issues relating to technology and future systems, but it did not produce results that could inform Army research and development. To accomplish this goal, the Army needs to embed technology seminar games in a more comprehensive process. At the start of the process, TRADOC should use Army's missions to derive a statement of desired capabilities. Then ASA(ALT) should produce lists of current and potentially available technologies that appear relevant. The ATSG should be a "brainstorming" session to project systems that would attain the desired capabilities by exploiting technologies. Specific scenarios are too distracting and confining for an exercise of this kind. It would be better to work simply from a statement of desired capabilities. TRADOC should sponsor force-building seminars that envision alternative future forces using the projected systems according to reasonably well-defined operational concepts. Finally, TRADOC should evaluate these future forces through wargaming.

CURRENT DESIGN

The teams were asked to deliberate on what can be characterized as an admixture of vignettes, capabilities, systems, and technologies. The vignettes were scenario snapshots intended to suggest future military requirements. These requirements drove selection of the

System Cards to be evaluated for each vignette. These evaluations presumably applied as well to the technologies underlying the systems. However, the connections formed by the teams between vignettes and requirements, between requirements and systems, and between systems and technologies were not clear, so it was not possible to identify audit trails from vignettes to technologies.

The ATSG used highly specific operational vignettes to spur the participants into thinking about the usefulness of projected systems. The vignettes created a strong link to the AAN wargame cycle. Each was drawn from one of the recently completed wargames, and several military participants were familiar with the incidents portrayed. However, the vignettes tended to be complex and at times obscured the players' rationale for making evaluations. One player summarized the problem in these words: "To me, the vignettes were distracting and limiting. I'm not sure why I gave the votes I did."

The vignettes also impelled the players toward an air-mechanized concept and away from any rival in two respects. First, most vignettes depicted successful operations by an air-mechanized force, implying that the Army was pursuing such a concept and believed it would be effective. Second, an air-mechanized concept was well represented in System Cards marked "AAN," while no rivals were as easily discernible. As a result, the players tended to vote for systems that supported an air-mechanized concept, even if they had misgivings.

Despite the fact that several of the System Cards provided to the players for their evaluation were either closely related or clear rivals to each other, the game format required each to be considered and evaluated separately. These procedural constraints limited what might have been a valuable discussion of the relative merits of systems best viewed as complements or rivals of each other. Furthermore, it was not always clear that the supporting technologies listed on the card were really technologies. In fact, some supporting technologies listed on the cards were listed as systems on other cards. This lack of a clear definition for the term "technology," as used in the game, led the players to focus more on the systems than on the enabling technologies. In addition, the large number of cards (67 originally) often compelled the players to make hasty, off-the-cuff evaluations.

RECOMMENDATIONS FOR IMPROVEMENT

The organizers of future seminars need to develop a set of capabilities distilled from multiple sources, including wargames. This set of capabilities should challenge participants to find ways of obtaining radically improved performance while leaving all reasonable alternatives open. It should not be based on any canonical view of how future Army forces should be structured or equipped. Doing this analytical work in advance will save participants' time and better focus their efforts.

The starting point for developing an appropriate list of force capabilities should be those missions that the Army will have to perform well into the conceivable future. From these missions, one can deduce the required capabilities. We offer the following definitions:

- **Mission:** broad description of an overall goal.

- **Capability:** power to accomplish a broadly defined task.

This definition of capability stresses the required attributes, and our revised definition of mission stresses its generic nature. For example, "Gain situational awareness" is considered to be a generic military mission. A required future capability might be the ability to present the commander with a fused common picture of the combat environment, including an assessment of risk.

The first step is to develop a set of generic military missions. Figure 4.1 lists the missions implied by the fifteen vignettes used in the ATSG. Some of these missions apply to several vignettes, suggesting that they might generate especially important requirements for future Army forces.

The next step in the process is to extract capabilities from the missions implied by the vignettes and other AAN study sources. It may be that capabilities already exist to accomplish the missions and what we seek are improvements. For example, the mission "Strike deep with precise fires" requires that the force be capable of accurately delivering munitions on target from great distances. Clearly, this is possible today with ATACMS. However, the mission may require improvements in accuracy, increases in range, or increases in lethality.

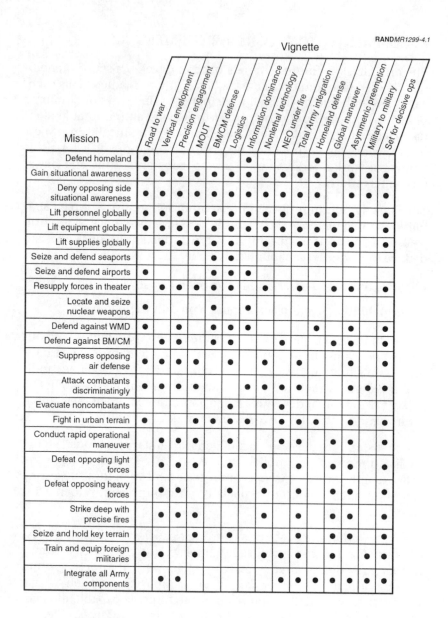

RAND*MR1299-4.1*

Vignette

Mission	Road to war	Vertical envelopment	Precision engagement	MOUT	BM/CM defense	Logistics	Information dominance	Nonlethal technology	NEO under fire	Total Army integration	Homeland defense	Global maneuver	Asymmetric preemption	Military to military	Set for decisive ops
Defend homeland	•						•				•		•		
Gain situational awareness	•	•	•	•	•	•	•	•	•	•	•	•	•	•	•
Deny opposing side situational awareness	•	•	•	•	•	•	•	•	•	•	•	•	•	•	•
Lift personnel globally	•	•	•	•	•	•	•	•	•	•	•	•			•
Lift equipment globally	•	•	•	•	•	•	•	•	•	•	•	•			•
Lift supplies globally		•	•	•	•	•			•	•	•	•			•
Seize and defend seaports					•	•									
Seize and defend airports	•				•	•	•								
Resupply forces in theater		•	•	•	•	•			•		•	•			•
Locate and seize nuclear weapons	•				•		•								
Defend against WMD	•		•		•	•	•				•		•		•
Defend against BM/CM		•	•		•	•			•		•	•			•
Suppress opposing air defense	•	•	•	•		•		•		•			•		
Attack combatants discriminatingly	•	•	•	•			•	•	•	•			•	•	•
Evacuate noncombatants						•			•						
Fight in urban terrain	•			•	•	•	•		•	•	•		•		•
Conduct rapid operational maneuver		•	•	•		•			•	•		•	•		•
Defeat opposing light forces		•	•	•		•		•		•		•	•		•
Defeat opposing heavy forces		•	•			•		•		•		•	•		•
Strike deep with precise fires		•	•	•			•		•			•	•		•
Seize and hold key terrain			•		•					•		•	•		•
Train and equip foreign militaries	•	•		•			•	•	•		•			•	•
Integrate all Army components		•	•						•	•	•	•	•	•	•

Figure 4.1—Generic Missions Abstracted from Vignettes

It is important to remember that a capability is not a system. By including systems in such a list, some technologies may be forestalled. In some cases, the military operators may consciously select a technological or systems option. For example, in support of the mission to lift equipment globally, one of the capabilities listed is "Improved roll-on-roll-off systems." The military operator in this case has chosen not to include systems that allow for equipment to be lifted out of a ship. This could be because it is inherently slower or because it requires specialized port handling equipment that may or may not be available. A complete list of these capabilities derived from the vignettes then becomes the starting point for encounters between military operators and technologists.

SYSTEMS SEMINAR

The systems seminar is essentially a "brainstorming" session. For brainstorming sessions to be productive, seminar planners must produce an environment that encourages the free flow of ideas. This means no preconceived notions of the "correct" military solution and no technological "pet rocks." A structure that is likely to prove successful has the following attributes:

- **Small.** The number of participants at any one session should be small: around 5 to 10. Large groups tend to produce one or two individuals who monopolize much of the meeting time and tend to intimidate less forceful participants. We observed this phenomenon at the ATSG.

- **Short.** All seminar meetings should be scheduled for one morning only. The participants are usually unable to stay creative, innovative, and focused for longer than four to five hours.

- **Focused.** Each session should focus on two or three related capabilities. This allows seminar planners to group technologists by field of expertise. It also allows for the seminars to "go on the road." That is, if maneuverability on land is the issue, it makes sense to hold the seminars in the Detroit area, which has perhaps the greatest access to automotive engineers.

Inputs/Outputs

The game inputs are the desired capabilities from the military opera-tors·and the technologies (not formally articulated) from the partici-pating engineers and scientists. The outputs are military systems. It is helpful in this context to think of a military system as a synthesis of capabilities and technologies (Figure 4.2).

The seminar participants are a significant part of the input mix. The military operators must be capable of articulating the desired force capabilities, and the scientists and engineers must be chosen because of their expertise in the requisite technologies. As part of the preparation process for the next seminar series, each of the capabili-ties derived from the AAN games and the existing vignettes should be expanded slightly to elaborate on the attributes particularly required to support military missions.

Process

The seminar itself is simple: two or three military operators articu-late the desired military capabilities, and the two or three researchers

RANDMR1299-4.2

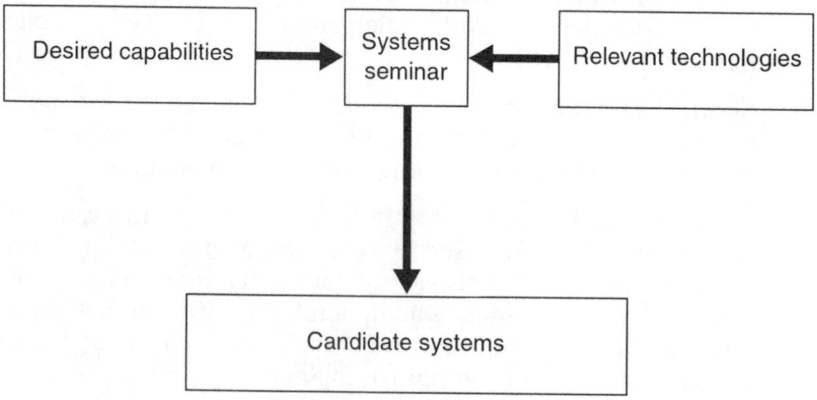

Figure 4.2—Capabilities, Technologies, Systems

respond with technological solutions. Properly executed, the technological solutions will suggest military systems to all participants, and the outcome of the process will be one or more candidate military systems.

It is likely that the systems suggested using this approach would be incomplete because of the narrow focus of the seminar. This is not a problem, in that other seminars on supporting capabilities will most likely fill in the gaps. In addition, it is likely that the group will expand its discussion beyond the scope of the subject capabilities, and this should not be discouraged.

There are several approaches the planners might take in running the seminars. All include running several (no more than five) seminars at the same time. One approach is to have each seminar deal with the same capabilities. This is especially useful if the process is "taken on the road." Another is to mix the capabilities among seminars so that several are addressed at once. This might be useful if the seminars are conducted in Washington. Another approach might be to assign connected capabilities to each seminar.

The process should be repeated several times, perhaps in a distributed fashion through the Internet. Iteration will help scientists and military officers identify promising technologies and exploit them in systems that meet military needs. The output of the systems seminars should be well-understood military systems exploiting current or projected technologies. Figure 4.3 illustrates the process using examples from the ATSG.

The outputs from the technology seminars form the basic input to the systems seminars. For example, the several systems included in the System Card set at the ATSG would qualify as candidate systems. Three of these are listed as inputs in Figure 4.3. Note that the sets can be characterized by systems that improve lethality, mobility, and protection.

As with the capabilities in the technology seminars, each candidate system should be described in sufficient detail to be understood by game participants. In particular, the enabling technologies for each should be made clear to the scientific participants. The military operations community should develop the system concepts, which must be consistent with the capabilities required of the future force.

RAND*MR1299-4.3*

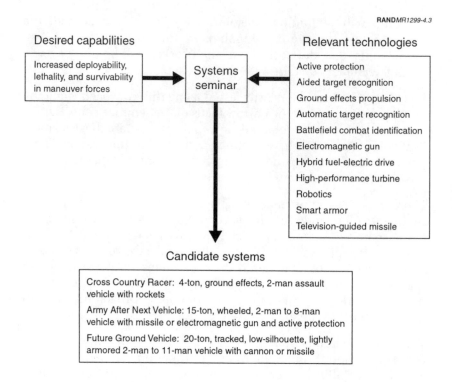

Desired capabilities

Increased deployability, lethality, and survivability in maneuver forces

Systems seminar

Relevant technologies

Active protection
Aided target recognition
Ground effects propulsion
Automatic target recognition
Battlefield combat identification
Electromagnetic gun
Hybrid fuel-electric drive
High-performance turbine
Robotics
Smart armor
Television-guided missile

Candidate systems

Cross Country Racer: 4-ton, ground effects, 2-man assault vehicle with rockets

Army After Next Vehicle: 15-ton, wheeled, 2-man to 8-man vehicle with missile or electromagnetic gun and active protection

Future Ground Vehicle: 20-ton, tracked, low-silhouette, lightly armored 2-man to 11-man vehicle with cannon or missile

Figure 4.3—Systems Seminar

Some examples of systems concepts are included in Figure 4.3. As with the system descriptions, the concepts must be clearly articulated and consistent with the missions and capabilities desired of the future force. An example of such a description is:

Army After Next (AAN) Vehicle. This is a light (c. 15-ton) combat vehicle designed to be transportable by the Joint Transport Rotorcraft (JTR). A family of AAN Vehicles includes variants optimized for command and control, armored combat, fire support, high mobility, recovery, reconnaissance, robotic engagement, and transport. Among the associated technologies (aggressive approach) are a compact kinetic energy missile, an electromagnetic gun, active protection against kinetic rounds, and smart armor.

FORCE-BUILDING SEMINARS

Force-building seminars explore how new operational concepts and new systems should be joined to design future forces.

Participants at this level should be Army operators familiar with Army doctrine and combat systems. Given that each system is essentially a military end item, the logical next step is to combine them, in conjunction with operational concepts for future forces, to produce alternative force designs. Figure 4.4 illustrates the process.

The input at the left consists of the candidate systems developed during the systems seminars. The input at the right consists of alternative operational concepts. These concepts may be suggested by the candidate systems in the light of desired capabilities and Army missions. In any case, there should be a clear understanding that a

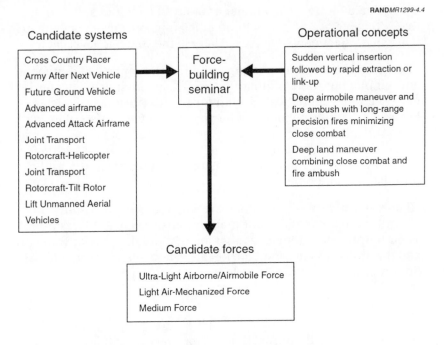

Figure 4.4—Force-Building Seminar

force design cannot be complete without both a well-defined structure and an operational concept.

The output of the process is candidate forces. In this example, we
depict three candidates, each associated with one of the three operational concepts. The force should be detailed enough to be represented in computer-assisted simulations. This means understanding
and quantifying the operational implications of the new or improved
technologies.

WARGAME

The last step in the cycle is to evaluate the alternative forces. One
approach is the annual strategic-level wargame traditionally held at
the Army War College together with supporting games played at
operational and tactical levels. The operational and tactical games
are designed to examine the tactical effectiveness of the force against
a postulated future enemy under a variety of conditions. The objective is to generate a series of outcomes from various engagements
that can be documented and used later in the strategic-level games.

The annual strategic-level wargame tests the impact of deploying
and employing the candidate future forces in specific scenarios
under certain geopolitical assumptions. This process is depicted in
Figure 4.5. The output of the strategic-level game consists of insights
on the effectiveness of the force given the assumptions and the scenario. Other insights and issues are possible as well, but with refer-
ence to the force, the emphasis is on the force structure and the
postulated operational concept.

High-level, free play wargames are not reproducible and cannot
attain experimental rigor, but their outputs are nevertheless useful.
Their output should include assessments revealing the advantages
and the drawbacks of candidate forces. This assessment should help
inform Army research and development.

OVERVIEW

Our recommended approach has three stages, each logically connected to the preceding stage. At its conclusion, TRADOC would

RAND*MR1299-4.5*

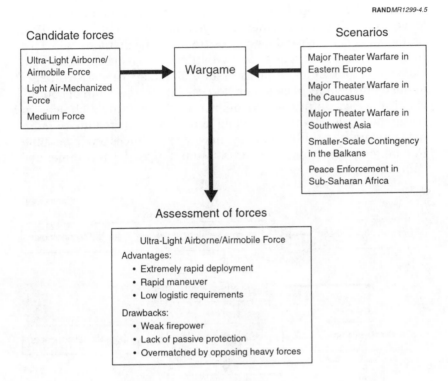

Figure 4.5—Wargame

have an audit trail extending from technologies to assessments of the likely performance of alternative future forces.

The initial inputs are a list of desired capabilities derived from relevant wargaming and other sources and a list of current and emerging technologies that might have military utility. During a systems seminar, operators and technologists draw together desired capabilities and relevant technologies to generate lists of candidate systems, broadly defined as major end items of military equipment. The next inputs are these candidate systems and operational concepts, essentially visions of how future forces might operate. During a force-building seminar, participants select candidate systems to realize operational concepts. They might also invent new concepts or modify the list of candidate systems to better realize a concept. The next inputs are these candidate forces and scenario sets intended to challenge them. During wargames and dynamically structured seminars, participants use the candidate forces to fulfill the missions called for by the scenarios. In doing so, the participants, usually including a cloistered group of impartial assessors, should arrive at assessments of the relative utility of candidate forces across a spectrum of contingencies. This output would help inform the Army's choices in research and development, leading to the eventual creation of more modern forces, including perhaps new types of forces made possible by emerging technologies. Figure 4.6 summarizes this recommended approach.

RANDMR1299-4.6

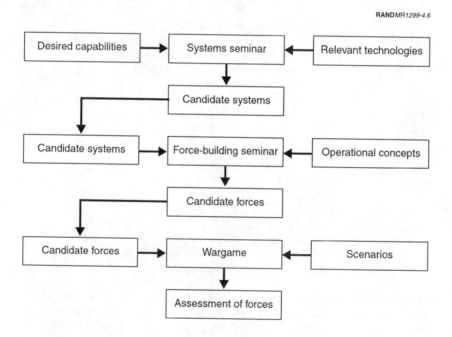

Figure 4.6—Overview of Approach

ANALYSIS OF SYSTEM CARDS BY KEY TECHNOLOGIES

This appendix presents a complete list of the System Cards, by function (C4ISR, operations, logistics). Each system is annotated to reflect its applicability across all subfunctions: C4ISR collection, transmission, and user systems; operations mobility, lethality, and survivability; logistics deployability and supportability.

Key Technology	C4ISR COL	C4ISR TRS	C4ISR USE	OPS MOB	OPS LETH	OPS SURV	LOG DEP	LOG SUP
Personnel pod						•		
Jet propulsion				•			•	
Advanced batteries	•	•	•	•		•		•
Electro-magnetic pulse protection	•	•	•			•	•	•
Smart structures	•				•	•	•	
Modular sensor packages	•							
Identification using multiple sensors	•		•					
Detection in foliage and clutter	•							
Sensor fusion	•		•					
Health and Monitoring System								•
Integrated biosensors	•					•		•
On-board prognostics								•
Auto target recognition and tracking	•				•			
Autonomous flight control	•			•			•	
Prime power for sensor packages	•							

Key Technology	C4ISR COL	C4ISR TRS	C4ISR USE	OPS MOB	OPS LETH	OPS SURV	LOG DEP	LOG SUP
Modular plug and play			•					•
High capacity data links		•						
Compact kinetic energy missiles					•			
High-powered microwave for offensive IW					•			
Extended range NLOS missile					•			
Electro-thermal gun					•			
Improved Stinger					•			
Electromagnetic gun					•			
Precision weapons with selectable warheads					•			•
Robotic fighters					•	•		
Ground vehicle mobility				•				
Turbine engine technology				•			•	
High efficiency diesel engine				•			•	•
Hybrid electric drive				•			•	•
Ceramic and active armor						•		
Multiplex/multimedia antenna		•						
Fuel cells				•			•	•
Hit/kill avoidance						•		
Signature reduction						•		
Tactical mobile robotics				•		•		
Ballistic protection						•		
Hyper-velocity missile gun					•			
Bio-sensitive crew environments						•		•
Electronic countermeasures	•	•	•		•	•		
Biomimetic armor materials						•		
Data processing for digital battlefield			•					•
System integration technologies	•	•	•					•
ISR vehicle technologies	•							
Distributed netted sensors	•							

Key Technology	C4ISR COL	C4ISR TRS	C4ISR USE	OPS MOB	OPS LETH	OPS SURV	LOG DEP	LOG SUP
Remote weather sensing	•		•	•		•	•	•
Health and Usage Monitoring System (HUMS)								•
Precision environmental control						•		•
Forward-Looking Infrared technology	•							
Phased array radars	•							
Battlefield Combat Identification	•		•					
Reduced vehicle and armor weight						•	•	
High altitude airborne precision insertion							•	
RAM air canopies							•	
Gliding decelerators				•			•	
Low fuel consumption auxiliary power						•		•
Autonomous soft landing system				•			•	
Soft landing airbag				•			•	
Advanced parachute materials				•			•	
Semi-rigid wing high glide capability				•			•	
Precision delivery with high glide wing				•			•	
Advanced guidance package for high glide wing				•			•	
Low observable active packages						•		
Microwave radar/FLIR sensor fusion	•		•					
Acoustic sensors	•							
Wire strike/obstacle detection				•		•		
IHPT and JTAGG				•				
All weather navigation				•			•	
Advanced drive system				•				
Rotary-wing structures technology				•			•	

Key Technology	C4ISR COL	C4ISR TRS	C4ISR USE	OPS MOB	OPS LETH	OPS SURV	LOG DEP	LOG SUP
Rotary-wing/composite wing simulation				•			•	
Composite-conformal arrays				•			•	
Advanced rotors				•			•	
Helicopter active controls				•			•	
Variable diameter tilt rotor				•			•	
Smart rotor system				•			•	
Rotary wing signature reduction						•		
IR signature suppression						•		
Full spectrum threat reduction						•		
Survivable/affordable airframe						•		
Autonomous camouflage						•		
Fold Tilt-rotor							•	
Variable geometry rotors				•			•	
Signature element tradeoff system						•		
Rotorcraft pilot associate				•			•	
Neural nets	•		•					•
Sensor collection management	•							
Smart process integration	•	•	•					•
Active databases			•					•
Tagging	•							•
Data mining			•					•
Virtual anchor desk								•
Information warfare protection	•	•	•			•	•	•
Multisensor control	•							
Distributed computing network	•	•	•					•
Rule-based processing			•					
Speech and text understanding			•					
Recognition, routing and analysis of data			•					•

Key Technology	C4ISR COL	C4ISR TRS	C4ISR USE	OPS MOB	OPS LETH	OPS SURV	LOG DEP	LOG SUP
Knowledge-based access, retrieval, integration			•					•
Display technology			•					•
Collaborative tools			•					•
Faster than real time modeling of courses of action			•					
Continually updating information priorities			•					
En-route mission planning			•					
System-on-system analysis			•					
Information filtering for situational awareness			•					
Automated C2 displays			•					
Built-in identification friend or foe			•					
Unattended ground sensors	•							
Anti-tampering technology/self-destruct						•		
Multi-mode warhead					•			
Self repair						•		•
Lock-on before launch					•			
Fire-and-forget					•			
Remote target designator link					•			
Dial-a-trajectory selectable targeting					•			
High-energy propellants					•			
All weather infrared seeker, fire and forget					•			
Hard target smart fuze					•			
Smokeless Propellant					•			
Miniature Electronic Time Set Fusing					•			
High Explosive Air-Bursting Munitions					•			
Chemical/gas pellets/other non-lethal application					•			
Advanced Composites						•		•
Ergonomic designs						•		
Signals intelligence	•							

Key Technology	C4ISR COL	C4ISR TRS	C4ISR USE	OPS MOB	OPS LETH	OPS SURV	LOG DEP	LOG SUP
New mensuration techniques	•							
Real time distributed object management	•		•					•
Automated data validation			•					•
Agents for intelligent inference			•					•
Intelligent object oriented maps			•					
Massively paralleled processors			•					•
Optical computing			•					•
Biological computing			•					•
Energy management								•
On-board electric generation system				•		•		
Microwave power				•				•
Micro-turbines				•				
Laser radar automatic target recognition			•					
Algorithms for synthetic aperture radar	•							
On-the-move automatic target recognition			•					
Distributed combat identification			•					
Production of biological materials								•
Production of non-biological materials								•
Ultraviolet particle sizer						•		
Miniaturized Detection Technologies						•		
Hand-Held biological warfare Agent Detector						•		
Automated DNA Diagnostic Sensor						•		
Laser Standoff Chemical Detection Technology						•		
Chemical imaging sensors						•		

Key Technology	C4ISR COL	C4ISR TRS	C4ISR USE	OPS MOB	OPS LETH	OPS SURV	LOG DEP	LOG SUP
Global integration of logistics information							•	•
Common operating environment software			•					•
High-reliability tracking of assets in transit							•	•
Quick response to changing destinations, priorities							•	
Intelligent Ammunition Supply Point							•	
Dynamic total asset availability prognostics								•
Smart skins and structures						•		
Real-time reporting of item condition codes								•
Database architecture			•					•
Protection from intrusions			•			•	•	•
EMP hardening	•	•	•			•	•	•
Embedded physical security	•	•	•			•	•	•
High Powered electro-magnetic pulse generation					•			
Controlled directional antenna airborne					•			
Composite chassis				•				•
Powered parafoil air delivery system				•			•	
Inflatable wing surface				•			•	
System monitoring								•
Fault tolerant information systems			•					•
Advanced network tracing and management		•						
Full use of firewalls at all levels of protocol	•	•	•			•		•
Virus elimination tools	•	•	•			•		•
Firewalls based on information-content	•	•	•			•		•
Multi-level security	•	•	•			•		•
Data authentication			•			•	•	•

Key Technology	C4ISR COL	C4ISR TRS	C4ISR USE	OPS MOB	OPS LETH	OPS SURV	LOG DEP	LOG SUP
Intrusion awareness			•			•		•
Database protection/reconstitution			•					•
Emissions shielding and protection	•	•	•			•	•	•
Automatic countermeasure recognition			•			•		
Self-defense network agent			•			•		•
Advanced encryption		•						
Robotic warehouse system								•
Surface ship electrical power system							•	
Ship turbine/diesel engines							•	
Ship Nuclear Power							•	
Ship Hybrid-electric power							•	
Materials and Processes for Corrosion Control							•	•
Surface Ship Integrated Top Side Concerns							•	
Advanced hull design for unencumbered sea state								
Wing design							•	
Sea state mitigation							•	
Hydrofoil							•	
Simulation-based design		•		•			•	
On-board self-protection							•	
Advanced materials and penetrators					•			
Miniaturized Guidance and Control Actuation					•			
Hypervelocity Missile Guidance					•			
Remote detonation control						•		
Self-disabling (programmable in fuse)					•	•		
Ballute detonation control					•			
Advanced materials for cargo protection							•	
Environmental controls on selected containers							•	

Key Technology	C4ISR COL	C4ISR TRS	C4ISR USE	OPS MOB	OPS LETH	OPS SURV	LOG DEP	LOG SUP
Self-healing, self-sealing skin structures						•	•	
Cargo diagnostics							•	
Shock-absorbing materials/crash resistance							•	
Advanced lightweight, high-strength materials							•	
Minimum touch packaging configuration							•	
Reduce bulk and weight of materials							•	•
Multifunction lasers					•			
Real time distributed software agents			•					•
Discrete, reliable determination of target hits					•			
Medium cannon technology					•			
Dual mode seekers					•			
Multipurpose improved munitions					•			
Semi-active suspension				•				
Convert kinetic energy hits to propulsive energy				•		•		
All dimension protection						•		
Increased reliability								•
Integrated beam control		•						
High power optical components					•			
Scaled adaptive optics and control systems					•			
Miniaturization of components								•
Low observable advanced materials						•		
Tele-operated positioning				•				
Embedded prognostics for refueling system								•
Embedded prognostics for MHE system								•

Key Technology	C4ISR COL	C4ISR TRS	C4ISR USE	OPS MOB	OPS LETH	OPS SURV	LOG DEP	LOG SUP
Fast-coupling refueling with combat vehicles								•
Embedded diagnostics for refueling system								•
Compact hydraulic lift/transfer system								•
Fuel cell exchange capability				•				•
Fuel bladder exchange capability				•				•
Ammo package exchange capability				•				•
Advanced spark suppressors						•		
Automated fuel status monitoring and reporting								•
Real-time inventory accounting and reporting								•
Variable velocity round					•			
Pellets with chem/gas for incapacitation					•			
Robotic companion				•		•		
Chemical Agent Prophylaxes						•		
Spray-on skin						•		
Bio Warfare Agent Confirmation Diagnostic Kit						•		
Joint Service Chemicals Miniature Agent Detector						•		
Chemical-biological Protective Duty Uniform						•		
Agent Impermeable Membranes						•		
Enhanced Respirator Filtration Technology						•		
Self-decontaminating chem/bio reactive surfaces						•		
Nanofibers						•		
Biomimetics						•		
Electro-spun nanolayering						•		

Key Technology	C4ISR COL	C4ISR TRS	C4ISR USE	OPS MOB	OPS LETH	OPS SURV	LOG DEP	LOG SUP
Smart skin for complete soldier chem/bio protection						•		
Microclimate cooling subsystem						•		
Medical countermeasures						•		
Advanced anti-convulsant						•		
Reactive Topical Skin Protectant/Decontaminant						•		
Automated pulmonary sensing and delivery						•		
Sustained-release chemoprophylaxis						•		
Immunity-enhancing pharmaceuticals						•		
Info warfare attack and protection			•		•			
Info operations identification friend or foe			•					
Multi-use unmanned aerial vehicles	•	•						
Planting viruses					•			
Helo active controls				•				
On-board plug in network				•				
Multi-spectral eye protection						•		
Stabilization for retinal displays						•		
Ultra Light Ballistically Resistant Materials						•		
Multifunctional Fabric Systems						•		
Individual Thermal Signature Reduction						•		
Extended component shelf life								•
Exoskeleton - aggressive						•		
Personal Communication System for the Soldier		•						
Personal Navigation and Reporting			•					

Key Technology	C4ISR COL	C4ISR TRS	C4ISR USE	OPS MOB	OPS LETH	OPS SURV	LOG DEP	LOG SUP
Wide angle beam steering		•						
Boresight, stability technologies					•			
Integrated photonic systems			•					
Broadcast-mode lasers		•						
Microelectro-mechanical Devices						•		•
Optoelectronics			•					
Burst transmit capability		•						
Wavelength agile lasers		•						
Advanced laser/RF communications		•						
Electronic Integrated Sensor Suite for Air Defense	•							
High-resolution bi-static radar	•							
Swarm of smart micro UAVs	•					•		
Short takeoff and landing				•			•	
Vertical takeoff and landing				•			•	
Integrated diagnostics/ modularized cargo pods							•	
Low cost, dual axis canard					•			
Low-cost strapdown mechanisms for PG					•			
Fiber Optic Gyro-Based Navigation Systems					•			
Vaccine delivery						•		
Genetically engineered vaccines						•		
Wearable biological detection system						•		
Vaccinology						•		
Biorepellents/ration supplements to repel vector						•		
Micro-air vehicles	•							
On-Demand Real-Time Video, Bio/Chem Sensing						•		

Key Technology	C4ISR COL	C4ISR TRS	C4ISR USE	OPS MOB	OPS LETH	OPS SURV	LOG DEP	LOG SUP
Vehicle and sensor stabilization	•							
Bio-recycling techniques								•
Water source detection techniques								•
Desalination Techniques								•
Improved Water Purification								•
"Still suit" capability in Land Warrior						•		•
Recover water from fuel cell byproducts								•
Water analysis system								•
Enhanced taste capability								•
Endothermal, disposable, chemical chiller								•
Advanced molecular sieves								•
Enzyme-eating purification								•
Through-Wall Sensing	•							
Audio Sensing	•							
Advanced night vision goggles					•			
Olfactory sensors					•			
Tele-robotic sensor EO/IR	•							
Semi-autonomous robotic spectral sensor	•							
Miniature sensor (e.g., "stick-to-the-wall")	•							
Nuclear sensors	•							
Millimeter wave communications		•						
Long endurance unmanned aerial vehicle	•	•						
Acoustic pressure wave generation					•			
Interference level resonance biological effects					•			
Directed micro-wave weapon (individual)					•			
Rapidly erectable barriers					•			

Key Technology	C4ISR COL	C4ISR TRS	C4ISR USE	OPS MOB	OPS LETH	OPS SURV	LOG DEP	LOG SUP
Foam materials					•			
Slippery agents					•			
Bonding agents					•			
Potential immobilization enhancers					•			
Air-bursting submunitions					•			
Multifunction propelling charge					•			
Wide area flash band					•			
Multiple effects with single delivery system					•			
Kinetic energy, direct fire, low hazard munitions					•			
Multiple tactical payloads					•			
Sticky foam and tire penetration					•			
Vehicle mounted microwave generator					•			
Portable EMP generator					•			
Direct injection high voltage discharge					•			
Spider fiber entangler					•			
Differential GPS			•					
Home on jam					•			
Home on spoof					•			
On-site manufacturing of parts								•
Hydrofoils and air-cushion vehicles							•	
Improved palletized and containerized cargo							•	
CHE/MHE extended operations							•	
Lightweight Airborne Multi-spectral Countermine						•		
Advanced Mine Detection Sensors						•		
Vehicle Mounted Mine Detection						•		

Key Technology	C4ISR COL	C4ISR TRS	C4ISR USE	OPS MOB	OPS LETH	OPS SURV	LOG DEP	LOG SUP
Seismic detectors	•							
Gas spectrum analysis	•							
Nitrogen in nuclei interrogation	•							
Tele-operated Ground Vehicle	•							
Integrated with robotic wingmen					•	•		
Ultra wide band RF impulse generator					•			
Increased flight efficiency				•				
Collision avoidance				•				
Space Object Identification	•							
Spaceborne combat Identification	•		•					
Satellite constellation reconstitution	•	•						
Satellite launch	•	•						
Weapons launch					•			
Satellite on demand	•	•						
Subscriber terminals with adjustable power		•						
Path diversity beam integration		•						
Low probability of inter-cept communications		•						
Solar-powered phone systems		•						
Optical up/down links		•						
Multi-Mission Space-Based Laser		•				•		
Adaptive Optics Mirror		•						
Laser Boresight Calibration		•						
Efficient Thrusters	•	•				•		•
Chemical resupply of space lasers								•
High Intensity pulsed UV light neutralization					•			
Enzymatic decontaminations						•		

Key Technology	C4ISR COL	C4ISR TRS	C4ISR USE	OPS MOB	OPS LETH	OPS SURV	LOG DEP	LOG SUP
Reduced weight of decontamination system						•		
Inflatable system for personnel protection						•		
Laminants to encapsulate contaminants						•		
Encapsulate radioactive materials						•		
High-speed shrink wrap for contaminants						•		
Dustbuster capability to clean spills						•		
Broad-spectrum non-toxin						•		
Counter-agent that eats contaminants/agents						•		
Satellites for communications and ISR	•	•						
UAVs for communications and IS	•	•						
Universal terminal		•						
Laser links UAVs to satellite		•						
Small antennas		•						
Smart antennas		•						
Self-healing networks		•						
Data warehousing			•					•
Information grid for C4ISR	•	•	•					
Anti-jamming for mobile units						•		
Self-opening networks			•					
Location independent personal addressing		•	•					•
Terahertz processors			•					
Collaborative interfaces			•					•
Intelligent agents			•					•
Cognitive interfaces			•					•
Reconstitution of critical functions						•		
Head-mounted, high resolution display			•					

Key Technology	C4ISR COL	C4ISR TRS	C4ISR USE	OPS MOB	OPS LETH	OPS SURV	LOG DEP	LOG SUP
Computer-Aided Diagnosis and Treatment						•		
Karnak glove - diagnosis						•		
Fluid replacement tech, e.g., synthetic blood						•		
Marker cards: smart "dogtags"						•		
Ministat casualty treatment						•		
Nano-surgeons						•		
Hybernation suspended animation						•		
Performance enhancers				•	•			
Atmospheric interceptors					•			
Hypersonic weapons					•			
Battlefield ordnance awareness								•
Hit-to-kill technologies					•			
On-board capability to kill attacking system					•			
Brilliant BBs: "escort defense"					•			
Broad band threat warning			•					
Combined transmission/ backscatter X-ray imaging						•		
Vehicle weigh-in-motion analysis						•		
Ion and Ion-trap mobility spectroscopy						•		
Fast-neutron interrogation system						•		
DNA matching for bio agents						•		
Robotic lifters						•		
embedded diagnostics						•		
Self-calibrating components						•		•
Battlefield repair								•
High-speed drop (no parachute)							•	
Self-moving mines					•			

Key Technology	C4ISR COL	C4ISR TRS	C4ISR USE	OPS MOB	OPS LETH	OPS SURV	LOG DEP	LOG SUP
Capability to produce deceptive effect						•		
	66	50	74	53	81	122	68	102

SAMPLE VIGNETTE

This appendix presents a sample vignette drawn from the set of fifteen used during the Army Technology Seminar Game. Each vignette presented (1) a statement of the situation, (2) mission, enemy troops, terrain-time-command and control (METT-T-C), (3) issues, and (4) an operational graphic.

VIGNETTE 1: ROAD TO WAR

Situation

An insurgency in Indonesia, the New Nationalist Movement (NNM), has fomented an international crisis. The NNM, Orange, is a very sophisticated and complex organization attempting to seize control of Sumatra and, ultimately, to gain control of the entire country of Indonesia. A pirate organization, the Sumatran Brotherhood, which is loosely affiliated with Orange, has acquired two 50-kiloton nuclear weapons and is transshipping them through Northern Sumatra (which is under Orange control). Orange has kidnapped some NGO workers of a humanitarian relief force in Sumatra.

METT-T-C

Mission: The United States authorizes a unilateral military operation to seize the nuclear weapons. This action leads to Orange counter actions that embroil the United States in a very complicated situation in Sumatra.

Enemy: Orange has the capabilities as listed:

- Brigade-size force of regulars–revolutionary guard.
- 2 brigades of Indonesian militia that have gone over to Orange.
- 2 brigades of national police that have gone over to Orange.
- 50,000 persons in commercial security organizations.
- 80-person terror unit.
- 1,000-person active (able to mobilize 10,000) direct action unit.
- 500-person special materials division (drugs, arms, WMD).
- 350 civilian ships.
- 50 civilian airplanes.
- Well-financed through legitimate business and criminal activity.
- High-tech scouts downlink satellite information in addition to traditional intelligence activities.
- Foreign information directorate lobbies for Orange.
- Media directorate develops and distributes Orange story.
- Political party (150,000 members) operates overseas offices.

Troops: Special forces units in country. Naval CVBG and Marine MEU at sea. Blue light battleforce and other special operations forces in CONUS.

Terrain: Northern Sumatra. Large urban center in Medan.

Time: September 2021. Expect nuclear weapons to be shipped out of Northern Sumatra within 48 hours.

Civilian: Minimize collateral damage. Do not engage Orange forces other than to recover nuclear weapons.

Issues

Blue must contend with the following issues:

- Global village of information shrinks timelines for action.
- Orange media blitz tailored and aimed at many audiences.

- Force protection against counterterrorism in CONUS.
- Coordination with allies and other nations in region.
- Information operations against sophisticated enemy.
- Permissive and nonpermissive NEO. Protection of U.S. citizens.
- Interagency efforts against enemy—seize financial assets, etc.
- Special operations direct action mission.
- Ability to influence military-to-military.
- Intelligence operations against "new" enemy.
- Ambiguity for enemy "center of gravity."
- Regional sensitivities to U.S. actions. U.S. ability to influence events.
- Overseas presence and power projection.

RAND*MR1299-4.7*

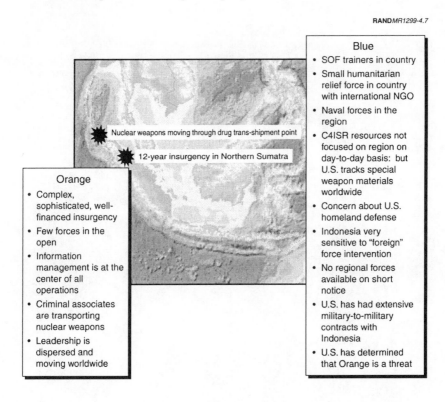

Blue
- SOF trainers in country
- Small humanitarian relief force in country with international NGO
- Naval forces in the region
- C4ISR resources not focused on region on day-to-day basis: but U.S. tracks special weapon materials worldwide
- Concern about U.S. homeland defense
- Indonesia very sensitive to "foreign" force intervention
- No regional forces available on short notice
- U.S. has had extensive military-to-military contracts with Indonesia
- U.S. has determined that Orange is a threat

Nuclear weapons moving through drug trans-shipment point

12-year insurgency in Northern Sumatra

Orange
- Complex, sophisticated, well-financed insurgency
- Few forces in the open
- Information management is at the center of all operations
- Criminal associates are transporting nuclear weapons
- Leadership is dispersed and moving worldwide

REFERENCES

Chairman, Joint Chiefs of Staff, *Department of Defense Dictionary of Military and Associated Terms*, Joint Pub 1-02, Washington, D.C., April 1998.

Birkler, John, C. Richard Neu, and Glenn Kent, *Gaining New Military Capability: An Experiment in Concept Development*, Santa Monica, CA: RAND, MR-912-OSD, 1998.

Darilek, Richard E., et al., *Surveying Relevant Emerging Technologies for the Army of the Future: Lessons from Forecast II*, Santa Monica, CA: RAND, R-35664-A, 1988.

Perry, Walter L., and Marc Dean Millot, *Army After Next: Winter Wargame Issues*, Santa Monica, CA: RAND, MR-988-A, 1998.

Perry, Walter L., Bruce Pirnie, and John Gordon IV, *Issues Raised During the 1998 Army After Next Spring Wargame*, Santa Monica, CA: RAND, MR 1023-A, 1999.

U.S. Army, *Army After Next Spring Wargame, State of the World 1998-2021*, Fort Monroe, VA: Training and Doctrine Command, April 19–30, 1998.

U.S. Army, *Army After Next 1998 Spring Wargame, Game Book*, Fort Monroe, VA: Training and Doctrine Command, April 19–30, 1998.

U.S. Army, *Analysis Plan for the Army After Next Spring Wargame 1998*, Fort Leavenworth, KS: TRADOC Analysis Center, April 8, 1998.

U.S. Army, Assistant Secretary of the Army for Research, Development, and Acquisition, *1998 Army Technology Seminar Game Report*, Washington, D.C.:   Science Applications International Corporation, 1999.